BRITANNICA BEGINNER BIOS

WILLIAM SHAKESPEARE

PLAYWRIGHT AND POET

DANIEL E. HARMON

Britannica®
Educational Publishing

IN ASSOCIATION WITH

ROSEN
EDUCATIONAL SERVICES

Published in 2018 by Britannica Educational Publishing (a trademark of Encyclopædia Britannica, Inc.) in association with The Rosen Publishing Group, Inc.
29 East 21st Street, New York, NY 10010

Distributed exclusively by Rosen Publishing.
To see additional Britannica Educational Publishing titles, go to rosenpublishing.com.

First Edition

Britannica Educational Publishing
J.E. Luebering: Executive Director, Core Editorial
Mary Rose McCudden: Editor, Britannica Student Encyclopedia

Rosen Publishing
Kathy Kuhtz Campbell: Senior Editor
Nelson Sá: Art Director
Brian Garvey: Series Designer
Ellina Litmanovich: Book Layout
Cindy Reiman: Photography Manager
Bruce Donnola: Photo Researcher

Cataloging-in-Publication Data

Names: Harmon, Daniel E., author.
Title: William Shakespeare: playwright and poet / Daniel E. Harmon.
Description: New York : Britannica Educational Publishing, in Association with Rosen Educational Services, 2018. | Series: Britannica beginner bios | Includes bibliographical references and index. | Audience: Grades 1–4.
Identifiers: ISBN 9781680488159 (library bound) | ISBN 9781680488142 (pbk.) | ISBN 9781538300237 (6 pack)
Subjects: LCSH: Shakespeare, William, 1564–1616—Juvenile literature. | Authors, English—Early modern, 1500–1700—Biography—Juvenile literature. | Dramatists, English—Early modern, 1500–1700—Biography—Juvenile literature.
Classification: LCC PR2895.H2665 2018 | DDC 822.3/3 [B]—dc23

Manufactured in the United States of America

Photo credits: Cover, p. 1 Stock Montage/Archive Photos/Getty Images; pp. 4, 27 Photos.com/Thinkstock; pp. 5, 24 GraphicaArtis/Archive Photos/Getty Images; p. 6 Jordan Pix/Getty Images; p. 7 S-F/Shutterstock.com; p. 9 David Hughes/Shutterstock.com; p. 10 AdstockRF; p. 11 Print Collector/Hulton Archive/Getty Images; p. 12 Peter Newark Pictures/Bridgeman Images; p. 13 Encyclopaedia Britannica, Inc.; p. 14 Oli Scarff/Getty Images; p. 16 Private Collection/Bridgeman Images; p. 18 National Portrait Gallery, London, UK/Bridgeman Images; p. 19 Universal History Archive/Universal Images Group/Getty Images; p. 21 Universal Images Group/Getty Images; p. 22 Culture Club/Hulton Archive/Getty Images; p. 28 Kathryn Scott Osler/Denver Post/Getty Images.

CONTENTS

CHAPTER ONE

WHO WAS WILLIAM SHAKESPEARE?

Hundreds of authors have written famous plays. Many of their works have been performed over and over, all around the world. The most famous of all those **PLAYWRIGHTS** is William Shakespeare.

Shakespeare is nicknamed the Bard of Avon. He was born near the river Avon in England and became that

MR. WILLIAM
SHAKESPEARES
COMEDIES,
HISTORIES, &
TRAGEDIES.
Published according to the True Originall Copies.

LONDON
y Ifaac Iaggard, and Ed. Blount. 1623

The first printed book of Shakespeare's collected works appeared in 1623. That was seven years after the playwright's death.

country's most famous poet, or bard. Although he began by writing poems, he soon turned his creative energy to writing plays. In all, he wrote some 38 plays and more than 150 poems. Some of his plays are comedies, some are tragedies, and some are histories.

In a scene from *Romeo and Juliet,* Romeo visits his sweetheart, Juliet, on her balcony. The play is one of the most famous of Shakespeare's tragedies.

Shakespeare's plays and poems remain popular worldwide. One reason is his cleverness with words. People often quote lines from his writings. These sayings can apply to different people

Quick Fact

Shakespeare earned little money by writing poems and plays. He became rich, though, because he owned part of the acting company that put on his plays.

Shakespeare's plays are performed all over the world. Here, Syrian children living in a Jordanian refugee camp act in a version of the play *King Lear.*

in different circumstances at different times in history. Another reason is his talent for creating believable characters. His plays also include fast action, suspense, and surprising twists.

CHAPTER TWO

A LAD BOUND FOR FAME

William Shakespeare was born in 1564 at Stratford-upon-Avon in Warwickshire, England. His birthday is celebrated on April 23, but the exact date of his birth is uncertain. In fact, little is known about his childhood. Stratford-upon-Avon, nestled

William Shakespeare was born in this house in Stratford-upon-Avon. His father made gloves and clothes for a living. Historians believe that William helped him for a time.

beside the river Avon, was a market town. English farmers, craftsmen, and traders from surrounding areas gathered in market towns to buy and sell.

William's father, John Shakespeare, made and sold gloves and other clothing. John was a town leader who eventually became BAILIFF. Will's mother, Mary, came from a wealthy family. Two older sisters died as babies, so young Will grew up as the oldest of six living children.

Will probably attended the local school. Besides English, he would have studied several foreign languages in the coming years. His later writings suggest he excelled in Latin. He also probably had his first tries at acting. Schools at the time used drama as a learning aid. Entering his teens, he may have acted in town plays.

Schools were located in buildings such as this one in Stratford-upon-Avon. Shakespeare is believed to have studied writing and various languages.

During this time, Will probably learned to make gloves and worked with his father. He may have planned to become a craftsman. In his spare time, he began to write poems and dramas.

When he was eighteen, William married Anne Hathaway, the daughter of a farmer from Shottery, near Stratford. She was eight years older than Will. They were living with his parents when their first child, Susanna, was born. Two years later, Anne had twins, whom they named Judith and Hamnet.

Practically nothing is recorded about the next seven years of Shakespeare's life. Some stories say he joined the English army or navy. Others say he might

Anne Hathaway's birthplace in Shottery is now a museum. The thatched cottage displays furniture and other items from the time when she and William lived.

have been a school-teacher or tutor. He might have been arrested and punished for poaching deer. He might simply have stayed in Stratford, helping in his father's business. Or he might have joined a TROUPE of traveling actors.

Quick Fact

Shakespeare began to earn a good income and notable respect in the London theater world. In 1596, he was able to obtain a coat of arms—a symbol of official recognition—for his father's family.

Literature and theater certainly had entered his blood. Sometime in the late 1580s Shakespeare left his family and settled in London, about 100 miles (160 kilometers) from Stratford-upon-Avon. Within a few years, he was making a name for himself as a poet and playwright—and not a completely favorable name. In 1592, a fellow playwright openly ridiculed him in a pamphlet.

Others who were involved in London theater and writing admired his works, though. He became quite successful during the 1590s.

> **Vocabulary**
>
> A **TROUPE** is a company of actors or stage performers. Members often travel to different locations to perform.

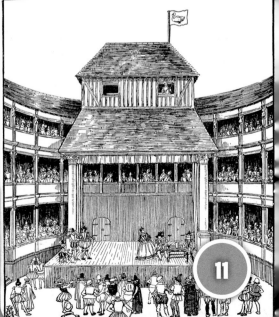

Troupes of traveling actors in Shakespeare's day probably played in theaters that looked much like this one. Theaters without roofs were common.

CHAPTER THREE

LONDON LIFE AND ENTERTAINMENT

It is not known how Shakespeare got started in the theater, but he probably gained experience as a member of an acting company. It is not certain exactly what duties he performed. He may have been mainly a stagehand, handling equipment and running errands. It seems likely that he

Much work went into preparing a play on a stage, then as now. This picture shows stagehands working while actors practice a play during the time of Shakespeare. Shakespeare may have started out as a stagehand.

was one of the writers for their scripts. He also may have been one of their actors, or at least a PROMPTER.

Shakespeare at first worked at two theaters outside the city wall. Both were managed by James Burbage. His son, Richard Burbage, was Shakespeare's friend and the greatest tragic actor of his day. Later, Shakespeare wrote and acted at various playhouses in the main theater district. More than a dozen theaters were active in

The buildings in red on this map mark the locations of theaters in and around London in about 1600. Shakespeare knew many of them well.

Vocabulary

A PROMPTER stands in the wings of the stage, unseen by the audience, and follows the script closely. The prompter helps actors who forget their lines.

than a dozen theaters were active in London. Some were set up in the yards of inns and taverns.

Theater companies regularly presented plays six days a week. Public theater buildings featured an open-air stage overlooking a courtyard. People who paid a small fee could stand in the courtyard to watch the play. In a ring surrounding this area were several stories of sheltered seating areas called galleries. People who paid more could sit in the seats. Plays had to be staged in daylight because there were no electric lights. And because there was no main roof, they could not be presented in winter.

People sitting in the sheltered galleries and standing before the stage watch actors perform *A Midsummer Night's Dream* at the new Globe Theatre in London in 2013.

Women in those times were not allowed to act in theaters. Teenage boys played their roles.

London in the 1590s was not exactly a pleasant place to live. Some 200,000 people were crowded into a rather limited space. There was constant activity. Many of the streets and alleys were filthy. People disposed of their waste simply by tossing it out into the open. Bandits, burglars, pickpockets, and other criminals were everywhere. Fights with swords and sticks frequently erupted in public, many of them deadly.

Quick Fact

Some parts of London in Shakespeare's time were very dangerous places to live and work. Shakespeare carried a sword for protection. Some actors and playwrights he knew were killed—or killed others— in sword fights.

London in many ways was a very unpleasant city. Here, a beggar is led through the streets by a rope and whipped from behind.

In 1592, a disease called the black plague devastated the city. Officials closed the theaters and other public places to stop its spread. Shakespeare then turned to writing poetry. During these years,

Shakespeare wrote his earliest sonnets and two long poems. Both were printed by Richard Field, a schoolmate from Stratford. These long poems were well received and helped establish Shakespeare as a poet. The theaters were reopened in 1594.

London was a center of world trade. Merchants brought their goods to sell from all over England and around the world. They arrived on foot, by oxcart, and by ship at the wharves on the river Thames. Shops thrived, selling every item imaginable.

Despite its dirtiness and dangers, Shakespeare loved living and working in London. Meanwhile, he kept ties with his hometown and family. In 1597, he bought a grand house for his family called New Place in Stratford-upon-Avon.

There was sadness in his life, too. His son, Hamnet, died in 1596 when the boy was just eleven years old.

CHAPTER FOUR

THE PLAYS

During the 1590s, Shakespeare became famous and wealthy. Anyone who enjoyed the theater was familiar with his plays. Many people did enjoy the theater. It was as popular then as movies and television are now. Many of Shakespeare's well-known lines were

This portrait of Shakespeare was painted in about 1610 when he was in his mid-forties. The picture is believed to have been painted from life.

In a scene from *Richard III*, Richard slyly speaks with Tyrrel, a killer, in a plot to have Richard's nephews murdered.

being quoted by people from all walks of life. The lines could apply to thousands of situations.

For example, a person in a hurry to get somewhere might shout, "My kingdom for a horse!" This was spoken by the frantic king in *Richard III*. To young people who are tempted to follow the crowd, wise parents might counsel, "To thine own self be true." This is from *Hamlet*. These and many other Shakespearean quotations are still used today.

Experts are not sure how many plays Shakespeare wrote or when each play was written. He wrote his plays to be acted, not read. Shakespeare took whatever

> ## Quick Fact
>
> Shakespeare wrote most of his plays for the Globe Theatre, which was completed in 1599. The theater has not survived, but a new Globe was built in 1997. It is very near the site of the original and was built to match the design of the original as much as possible.

took whatever forms were attracting attention and made them better. To save time he borrowed basic plots from other works. Sometimes Shakespeare expanded and adapted old stories, while sometimes he worked with more recent tales.

Titus Andronicus was the first tragedy Shakespeare wrote, but it is not the best known. Much more famous are *Romeo and Juliet*, *Macbeth*, and *Hamlet*. *Romeo and Juliet* is about two young lovers who secretly marry even though their families are enemies. Their plans for a happy life go horribly wrong. *Macbeth* is about a

Scottish general who murders others to gain and keep power. He is eventually killed. In *Hamlet*, the main character seeks **REVENGE** for his father, who was murdered by Hamlet's uncle.

Among Shakespeare's romantic comedies, *A Midsummer Night's Dream* is one of the most successful. The plot revolves around various couples, engagements, and mix-ups in a forest filled with fairies. Other comedies include *Twelfth Night*, *The*

Hamlet and two companions encounter the ghost of his father, the murdered king, in *Hamlet*. This is one of Shakespeare's best-known tragedies.

Comedy of Errors, and *Much Ado About Nothing.* *Twelfth Night* uses the DEVICE of mistaken identities. A shipwreck begins this play full of disguises and unreturned love. *The Comedy of Errors* also uses

the device of mistaken identities, this time involving two sets of identical twins. *Much Ado About Nothing* is a love story complicated by lies, insults, and tricks.

Puck (*left*) is a mischievous fairy in the play *A Midsummer Night's Dream.* Puck is sent by the angry fairy king Oberon to create confusion in the love relationships of other characters.

> **Vocabulary**
>
> A literary **DEVICE** is an element such as a misunderstanding or a moment of suspense that the author uses to create a dramatic effect.

Shakespeare's noted historical plays include *Richard III*, *Henry IV*, and *Henry V*. Each of the leading characters was a king of England.

Only about half of Shakespeare's plays were published during his lifetime. These were published in quarto form. This means they were printed on both sides of large sheets of paper with four printed pages on each side. The sheets were folded up to make the pages of a book.

CHAPTER FIVE

SUCCESS AND LASTING FAME

Shakespeare became one of the most famous people of his day. In London, his admirers included Queen Elizabeth I and later King James I. Shakespeare's companies performed for them and their COURTS. His plays were popular throughout Europe.

Shakespeare (*center*) and the Lord Chamberlain's Men perform *Two Gentlemen of Verona* for Queen Elizabeth I (*right*), seated beneath the royal canopy, or cloth covering.

Vocabulary

A royal **COURT** was the great chamber where a king or queen did business each day. People who regularly appeared at court included advisers and government officers, as well as some of the king's or queen's relatives and favorite people.

Shakespeare was not just a writer. He was also a member and part owner of one of the main theatrical companies in London, the Lord Chamberlain's Men. When Queen Elizabeth died in 1603 she was succeeded by King James. He greatly enjoyed the theater and made the Lord Chamberlain's Men his official performing company. They became known as the King's Men.

A few years later, the King's Men began performing at Blackfriars, one of London's indoor theaters. At roofed theaters, companies could perform year-round, not just during the warm months. Blackfriars was a

> **Vocabulary**
>
> **PROFITS** are the money earned from a business after paying for the expenses of the business.

private theater. Admission was expensive, and only well-to-do people attended.

Shakespeare is not known to have acted after 1603. He focused his time and energy on writing and on running the theatrical company. He received a share of the **PROFITS**, making him financially secure.

One of Shakespeare's last plays was *The Tempest*. It is about an Italian nobleman who is thrown from power by his evil brother and stranded on an island with his daughter. The nobleman possesses magical abilities, which he uses to right the wrongs against him.

In about 1612, Shakespeare left London and retired to Stratford-upon-Avon. The following year, the Globe Theatre burned. He helped in the building of

Beginning in 1599, Shakespeare's plays were produced at the Globe Theatre. It was located on the south bank of the Thames.

the new Globe. Shakespeare died in Stratford on April 23, 1616. He was fifty-two years old.

Although details about his life are not well known, William Shakespeare is one of the most famous people in history. His plays continue to be as popular today as

Quick Fact

Many historians believe William Shakespeare died on his birthday, although the exact date of his birth was not recorded.

A theater company from Colorado uses a scene from *Twelfth Night*, with its harsh Malvolio character, to teach school students about cyber-bullying.

they were during his lifetime. They have been translated into every major modern language. They are performed regularly on major stages around the world. They also are popular in school and community theaters.

People from around the world travel to Stratford-upon-Avon to see where Shakespeare grew up. The house where he was born still exists. The Royal Shakespeare Theater is a popular destination as well.

1564: William Shakespeare is born at Stratford-upon-Avon in Warwickshire, England.

1582: William marries Anne Hathaway.

1583: Their first child, Susanna, is born.

1585: Twins, Hamnet and Judith, are born to William and Anne.

1592: The plague sweeps London, forcing theaters to close.

1594: London theaters reopen. At about this time, Shakespeare joins the Lord Chamberlain's Men.

1596: Shakespeare's son dies.

1599: The Globe Theatre is completed.

1603: Queen Elizabeth I dies and is succeeded by her cousin, King James I. Shakespeare's theatrical company, Lord Chamberlain's Men, becomes the King's Men.

1608: The King's Men begin performing at Blackfriars, an indoor theater in London.

1609: A book of Shakespeare's sonnets is published.

1612: Shakespeare returns to Stratford-upon-Avon to live.

1616: Shakespeare dies in Stratford-upon-Avon.

GLOSSARY

COMEDY A funny play, story, poem, film, or other form of entertainment.

DRAMA A play or other form of entertainment that involves conflicts, emotions, or other serious elements.

ERRAND A short trip to obtain or deliver an item or conduct brief business.

EXCEL To do better than others.

FRANTIC Severely worried, desperate.

LITERATURE Written works including plays, books, and poems.

PLOT The basic story told in a play or other literary work.

POACH To hunt illegally on private property.

RIDICULE To make fun of.

SCRIPT The written text of a stage play.

SONNET A form of rhyming poem consisting of fourteen lines.

SYMBOL A sign or token that represents a person, item, or cause.

TAVERN A public place where customers are served alcoholic drinks.

TRAGEDY A play or other literary work that ends in a main character's death or ruin.

TUTOR One who instructs an individual student rather than a class.

WHARF (plural **wharves**) A wooden platform at the edge of a waterway where ships are loaded and unloaded.

BOOKS

Carew-Miller, Anna. *William Shakespeare: Great English Playwright & Poet* (People of Importance). Broomall, PA: Mason Crest, 2014.

Chrisp, Peter, and Steve Teague. *Eyewitness Shakespeare*. New York, NY: DK Publishing, 2015.

Johnson, Robin. *William Shakespeare*. New York, NY: Crabtree Publishing Company, 2016.

Manning, Mick, and Brita Granström. *William Shakespeare: Scenes from the Life of the World's Greatest Writer*. London, UK: Frances Lincoln Children's Books, 2015.

Williams, Marcia. *Tales from Shakespeare*. London, UK: Walker Books, 2015.

WEBSITES

Because of the changing nature of internet links, Rosen Publishing has developed an online list of websites related to the subject of this book. This site is updated regularly. Please use this link to access the list:

http://www.rosenlinks.com/BBB/Shakespeare

INDEX